The Nature of God

A Kingdom's Perspective

The Nature of God

A Kingdom's Perspective

Frankie L. Jackson

The Nature of God
A Kingdom's Perspective

 Published by **End Time Wave Publications,** P.O. Box 670, Bloomingburg, NY 12721.

ISBN 978-1-889389-35-6

Note: In some Scripture quotations, italics have been added by the author for emphasis only.

Table of Contents

Preface

Some people today think of God as being a harsh taskmaster who is distant from them. God may be looked upon as a mean tyrant who has made up many rules to keep us from enjoying life. Such false concepts of God adversely affect one's relationship with God. Assuming God to be cold and exacting then it becomes difficult, perhaps even impossible to really love God as we should. Our lives then might be lived in unholy fear. Understanding God as a kind and understanding God will make our inner life likely to reflect that concept. Many people today, including some Christians are plagued with an improper concept of God and as a result they are very unhappy and grim. When Christians live like this they misrepresent the true nature of God. Also, a distorted notion of the nature of God may make one reason that there is no way one can please God. So why even bother to try. Therefore, many don't try and end up wasting their lives.

Do you really know God as described in the Bible? What is your concept of the nature of God? It is vitally important to the way you live.

Our concept of God controls our level of relationship with Him. If our understanding of God's nature is poor or limited we will have a low level of relationship with Him. Knowledge of God should therefore be based on a personal encounter with God. How can we truthfully know God's nature without honestly seeking to know Him? To know God's nature is to seek to know the very essence of God. Honestly, we often make assumptions about the nature of God without really knowing Him. We have a perception about God. However, that perception changes as we get to know Him.

God is King. To know Him we must first seek to be in His Kingdom and how He rules His Kingdom. As long as we live outside God's Kingdom, our perception of the King will be distorted until we become part of the Kingdom of God to learn His ways. God's nature is His absolute glory and essence. The nature of God can be looked at through His laws and principles. God's nature will never change. The only thing that changes is our perception of Him.

I have been living in the Kingdom of God for sometime now. Thinking about how to present this book to you from the point of view of an insider has not been an easy one. What I will like you to know as you embark on the journey of rediscovering the nature of God from a Kingdom's perspective is that God endow you with understanding and may He visit you as you read along. I may not expressly mention the word kingdom as you read along because I am writing as a citizen of the Kingdom of God. It is my hope that you also see yourself as a citizen of the Kingdom of God. God bless you.

Pastor Frankie Jackson
July 2007

Introduction

Have you ever wondered why in between the many human assumptions of the "Nature of God" we sometimes become perplexed and are rather left with many unanswered questions? Man's innate longing and pursuit to know and understand things beyond his physical sense has today become acute. Many of the questions that we tend to ask are simply reflections of how we perceive God. Consequently, we have given a spectrum of meanings, many of which are strange to the Bible, the word of God.

This shows the importance of having the proper knowledge about the Nature of God. As I gleaned around, I discovered that the issue at hand is much deeper than one may think. Many of the ways we perceive the Nature of God doesn't seem to lend themselves to a coherent picture. We have put him in a box so that we can study him and draw our own conclusions about his nature.

The Bible however, communicates a true picture of God and gives us the master key to knowing Him. God declares in Isaiah 46:9-10 "*... Remember the former things of old: for I am God, and there is none else like me, declaring the end from the beginning, and from ancient times the things that are not yet done, saying, My counsel shall stand, and I will do all my pleasure...*"

The increasing exposure of today's society to scientific influence with an atheistic bias has resulted in emphasis being placed exclusively on questioning the very existence of God. This has rather tended to heighten the skepticism of many people about the existence of God. Thus the very subject about the discussion of the Nature of God is relegated to the background. Even if it is discussed, it is done with the view of predator and prey.

One of the limitless confidences one can have in the Bible is its complete inspiration and final authority. While it does not tell us all we would like to know about the Nature of God, it does reveal all of what we need to know.

There are five essential keys to reaping the full abundance of God. These keys reveal a deeper knowledge of "God's Method of Operation (GMO). That is, how God operates and thinks. We place limits on ourselves when we do not challenge ourselves to dig deep in the word of God to understand Him as He would have us understand Him. What we do not know will limit how much we can ask for, and thus limit our options in benefitting from whatever is made available to us. This is why there must be a paradigm shift in our thinking (perception) in the way we think of and approach God. *God looked down from heaven upon the children of men, to see if there were any that did understand, that did seek God (Psalms 53:2).* There are levels of understanding. God meets us at our own individual level of understanding. As long as we do not seek to know deeper than we know and understand Him better than we do today, we will always be met at our current level of understanding.

To know God is to understand all there is to know about Him. For example, how he thinks, acts, his priorities, his goals, etc. To fully know Him is to approach life from His viewpoint and see things as He does; become like Him and do what He does. The Bible invites and even urges each one of us, to know him intimately, personally and deeply. You can embark on a journey that leads to knowing God. God is King and so we must know him from the perspective of a kingdom. This book takes you on a journey to knowing the Nature of God from a *Kingdom's Perspective.*

Chapter 1

God's Intent vs. Man's Perception

Design Intent vs. Perception

There exists thousands of works designed by different designers. Each designer had an intent which is generally called the *design intent*. The design intent can be known if the design of the designer is correctly read and interpreted. For the design intent to be properly understood the design information must be processed. The act of processing the available information is called *perception*. What is perceived to be the intent of the designer does not necessarily mean what the designer actually intended. To understand what the designer intended it is important to be properly trained to read designs. For example if you are not trained to read and understand architectural designs you will not know why an architect chooses to make a wall as thick as 5 inches (to withstand the weight it has to bear) in a building he designed. You will definitely misread it or you may assume that a 5 inch wall cost too much. To save money you reduce the wall thickness to 2 inches. The wall may collapse in a short time and you will have to spend an additional time and more money in reconstructing it. In the end you loose because you failed to correctly perceive the design intent of the architect for the 5 inch wall.

This brief example helps us to understand that *misconceptions arise because of the wrong perceptions*! Note that all the while the design intent of the architect for the 5 inch wall has remained the same. The problem arose because of the wrong perception of the architect's design intent. It is because of this same wrong perception why people refer to some of Job's quotes in the Old Testament that, "Though He slay Me I will trust in Him" and "It's the Lord that taketh away" (Job 9:12, 13:15). The argument here is that many peoples perception is that it is the Lord that gives and takes away. The problem with this kind of thinking is clear, wrong perception of the design intent of God! As earthly parents we should ask ourselves this question. I wonder how an earthly father will give to his children and then take it back to destroy it so his children will suffer. Do you design and build a computer only to destroy it before it gets to the market? No I guess. Otherwise computers will not exist because they all have been destroyed by their designers.

Natural and Spiritual Laws of the Designer

For a design to work the way it was intended by the designer's design intent, it must obey all the laws (rules) that govern the intent. For example a fish was designed to live and abide by the laws of the sea and cannot live outside water. Thus for it to survive as a fish it must live in the water. In a similar fashion God made *natural* and *spiritual* laws to govern natural things before He put man on this earth. While the angles, devils and demons are subject to only spiritual laws, man is subject to both the natural and the spiritual laws because he is naturally and spiritually designed.

Natural Laws are Predetermined

The cycles of nature and history constantly repeat themselves (Genesis 1:11-14) and go round in circles. The book of Ecclesiastes says "*there is nothing new!* All the discoveries about everything we know today existed before God put man on the earth. In short, every fruit or tree, for example, the orange and watermelon we know today have predetermined laws that govern them, even their genetic makeup. Their colors, size, pigmentation, taste and types of seeds they produce have already been predetermined by God (Genesis 1:12). This is why oranges hang on trees while watermelons creep on the ground because of its weight. (it weighs as much as 25 to 50 pounds).

As a boy like many other kids I was fascinated by the character superman and could not comprehend how he could defy the laws of gravity. My fascination with the feats of superman made me decide I could also defy the laws of gravity. After several practice jumps off of my mother's sofa I concluded I'm ready to fly. I chose the next door neighbor flat roof as the place for my daring feat. The position seemed perfect I said to myself, because my mother would not see me through her kitchen window. Using a huge towel (without my mother's permission) as a cape, I jumped off the roof. I went down so fast and hit the surface so hard that, I immediately began to appreciate the laws of gravity. What I discovered besides a bruised backside was that the laws of gravity did not change. God made some creatures to disobey the laws of gravity. They have a mechanism for taking off the ground and landing wherever they please. I did not have any mechanism for that and my ignorance did not make me exempt from the bruises. Like in the case with the architect, it was me who had the wrong perception.

Man's Perception of God

I have earlier on stated that misconceptions give rise to wrong perception. If we have poor understanding of God's nature, we misconstrued His acts to be His nature. Indeed, we try to make Him fit into our limited perceptions. This then takes control of us and we preach it as the real. In fact, because perception is the act of information processing, it is only done through the senses. It also means perception is knowledge derived through one of the senses.

Earlier on I mentioned that what is perceived might not necessarily mean what the designer intended. This means that our senses may or may not perceive what is intended from the information available. Throughout the Bible, numerous examples of correct and wrong perceptions exist. In Galatians 2: 9 James, Cephas and John correctly perceived the grace given to Paul by God, and so they gave him and Barnabas the right hand of fellowship. Another situation of correct perception is found in Acts 10:34.

A situation with the wrong perception is when James and John nick named "sons of thunder" (Luke 9: 53-56), asked if Jesus will command fire to consume those who did not receive him. They had perceived Jesus Christ to be somebody interested in showing his power through wrath and destruction. Jesus' rebuke of them was that they did not know what their true nature was. For their nature is to be the nature of God (to save lives, not destroy them). Other are the case of the Samaritan woman at the well (John 4:7-19) and that of Simon (the sorcerer) in the book of Acts (Acts 8:13, 18-22).

The thing here is that man has a problem understanding what *sort* of being God is. Because we have assumed that God's mind is like our own minds, we tend to think that He will only decide something or have a strong feeling that causes Him to act out of excitement or anger. God however, is not such. What we fail to recognize here is that God is beyond the comprehension of finite man. For to think of him this way is like putting him in a box, inferring in the process that God is but as fallible and human as his creatures. Other ways we try to do this is to use religious conceptions as a tool to attempt to perceive the nature of God. In so doing man has rather tended to speculate and is left with only questions that have gone unanswered. Questions such as 'who really is God?" Clearly, it is just a reflection of the how man perceives God. The result is the multiplicity of the meanings of the word of God, many of which are foreign to the Bible.

Chapter 2

The Truth About God's Nature

At this point you might have come to realize that there is value in spending some time contemplating about God's nature. There is of course a lot being discussed about whether the nature of God is some imaginary thought. Sometimes it is talked about as if it is a figment of human imagination or a human invention. Still others may think the nature of God is not to be taken seriously. This is the more reason why we must take a closer look at this issue. With the scripture in hand we contemplate on the nature of God; it enables us to view things from the perspective of a Holy God. Not a smoggy world like perception. In knowing the truth about the nature of God, we will be able to cope with the exigencies of life. For since the creation of the world God's divine nature has been clearly seen, being understood from what has been made (Romans 1:20).

In this chapter I will focus on four areas that will greatly help in understanding the truth about God's Nature. The four areas I will be focusing on are:

1. Knowing God's Nature through His actions.

2. God's Right to make demands on His creation.
3. God is positioned to make anything possible for us.
4. God put in us to be like Him.

Knowing God's Nature through His Actions

God is a God who can be known personally. Because He is knowable, He wants to be known. This is why it is possible to know Him through His actions. You may or may not agree with this point. But let us look at it this way. I am sure you will agree with the fact that to some degree the character of every author can be judged from what we read of his works. It is the same way that we can judge the manifold works of God from what we see all around us, be it past, present, physical or spiritual. So you will agree that we see and know God as manifested in his activities in the whole world around us. Nothing on earth happens without his saying so.

Just take a look at an ordinary leaf of a tree. Is it not a marvel that there are over a billion different kinds of them? Another example is the eye of an insect which has over a thousand million pieces of sections to differentiate size, shape and color of any object.

God's Right to make demands upon His creation

Before you disagree with this topic, I would like to draw your attention to Luke 19:11-22, 1 Corinthians. 9:11 and Mark 11:12-14. I am definitely hoping that you read these passages and understood them. If not I will suggest you read it once again. First God created mankind and put him on earth and gave him the authority to rule the earth. This makes mankind accountable to God. Right? Good! We are getting closer!

God gave laws and advice to mankind, taught him how to live and how to make his own medicine and to get his own food. Because everything man does or will do has or will have an impact on life or non-life forms, he was told that he was solely held responsible for any action of his; for to demand is to ask with authority. In Genesis 9:1-6 God again tells Noah that he will make demands for any murder committed by man or beast. He established once again the responsibility to populate the earth.

God is positioned to make anything possible for us

Opportunities open up when the right relationship between two people exist. For most of us we expect to be accepted, loved and cared for not just with superficial words. This is because of the expectation that the care and concern will be proven by their actions. It helps in deriving a sense of purpose for our very existence. It improves our relationships and helps us to look forward to surviving for our next project. This is the same thing that will happen when we relate to God. In a moment by moment relationship, He can direct every step we make or have to make so that we can do what's in our best interest and what pleases Him at all times.

For most, love, care and acceptance help us to find fulfillment in life. It is the quench for the thirst that yearns within us. Therefore it is great to know that we have a God who satisfies that thirst and brings a sense of constant satisfaction. Most times we make plans and do things with positive expectations. Unfortunately we quickly forget that we don't have comfort over all the circumstances of life. Because of this uncontrollable circumstance of life, it behooves on us to learn to trust God; for with God all things are possible (Mt 19:26). When God is left out we tend to lapse into the discouragement of different circumstances.

Cheap lies of flattery, ritual praise, insincere words repeated over and over without regret for what is really happening push aside the fact that it is in the nature of God to love honest talk. When this happens, our relationship with God becomes cluttered with disagreements, struggles with different situations of life and different conflicts of life. The conclusion one can draw from such picture is the perspective of looking through a pinhole where the entire picture cannot be seen.

God has the ability to help and understand us. He works for us and does things for us all the time. So He has the ability to handle our situations. What we have to do is written in Ps. 37:4, 5.

God put in us to be like Him

Gen.1:26-27 tells us that man was created in the image and likeness of God. Right? If this is true, then that would mean all the billions of people look like God! Since we all look physically different it is obvious that the image and likeness has not much to do with the physical. You see if we share physical appearance with God, then God should be a "twin" or your "twin". Right? The clue to this verse is the characteristics we share with God, because we all agree that people can share similar characteristics without sharing physical appearance or features. God breathed into man His very essence so that he could look like Him forever beyond mere death.

Take a look at the situation on the lake (Luke 8:22-25). Jesus and His disciples were crossing the sea when a storm threatened to upset and sink their boat. The disciples were afraid while Jesus was fast asleep at the bottom of the deck. So they called Jesus and He in turn rebuked the wind.

The disciples wondered what manner of man Jesus was. Because Jesus knew who He was He solved the problem. The disciples however did not know who *they* were. That is a problem we still have today. We don't see greatness inside of us. However, God sees it. He put it there. Is it any wonder that David would ask why God was so mindful of man (Ps.8:4-6)?

I have already mentioned that man being in the image of God exists in the spiritual personality and not so much the physical. God having dominion over everything gave dominion to man to exercise authority (Gen.1:26-27). This is why Jesus told the sons of thunder that they know not what spirit they are made of (Lk.9:55). God having made the earth and its fullness gave Adam dominion over all his works. Thus becoming the "god of this world" just as "God is God of the universe."

Chapter 3

The Character of God

If your survival is dependent on someone other than yourself, then you better know his or her character. This is because every action of his/hers will determine your welfare and future. Since character motivates actions, it would be better for you not to speculate his/her true character so as not to cause yourself confusion, delusion and disappointment. Rather knowing and understanding his/her true character will take away the "why" or the "what if" of all problems. If you understood this then you need to know that knowing and understanding the character of God is essential since we are totally dependent on Him for our existence and survival. The reason for our failure to see how dependent we are upon the character of God is the decades, if not centuries of misinformation and unnecessary speculation, and because of that we tend to doubt the motives of God. What we have to understand here is that the motives of God are absolutely what is best for us in His supreme will. God's character can always be seen in His distinctive qualities.

God's desires toward mankind are not the same desires of man to man. For example, your friend may be ill or in need of salvation, but you can neither heal him nor save him. To be precise, there is little you can do about it. Even if you are a medical doctor you can only administer medicine, but how the healing will take place is beyond your imagination and so you would have to depend on God for your friend's healing. For a God who is omnipotent, He has the power to achieve everything He desires. Just as He desires us to be kind and gentle towards one another, He desires that all men be saved and to come to the knowledge of the truth (1Tim.2:3, 4). God desires that all men obey His commands (Acts 17: 30).

God's nature as we notice also is in His benevolent attitude toward mankind which results in favor granted mankind by God. We do not deserve God's grace and we have not earned it either. It was mans choice to rebel against God. As if it is not enough, we continue to rebel knowingly or unknowingly. God did not force us to sin. It is all around us. Yesterday's headline had sin all over it. Today's and tomorrow's headlines will definitely have sin still in them. Sin seems to have all the fun today. It is at our expense. Man's life is such that it continuously expresses evil, doing every unthinkable wicked thing that man's passions and evil thoughts lead to. Because of the merciful nature and character of God hope is not lost. Rebellious as we are God's compassionate nature caused Him to give us back our lives (Eph.2: 3-5) through the death of His son (Jn.3:16).

God's nature shows His fatherly character (2 Cor.6: 18). He guides us (Ps.25:10, Ps.32:8, Jn.16:13) in all ways and in all things. He is a preserve of our soul and preserves us from all kinds of harm that may come from the devil (Ps.12: 7-8, Jn.10:10, 17:15). As a father He is our daily provider (Ps.23; 1, 37:25, Mat.6: 26-34, 2Cor.9:6-15), and saved us from the ultimate death (Ps.3: 8, Jn.3:16-21, 1Cor.1:18-21, Eph.1:4-10, 2Tim.1: 9-10) which was the result of our sins.

When God created the world He didn't leave man alone to face all the difficulties, challenges and responsibilities. He related to man in all his ways, advising, cautioning, conversing and having a good relationship with man. God never remain aloof from the pain and suffering that man was going through. That is why he sent His Son here on earth to get us out of the mess and troubles we find ourselves in. Because words don't communicate care and concerns much as action do. God sent Jesus so that through His death His love, care and concern can be demonstrated in action. This way we would come to know His nature and character very well.

Now that I have explained what the character of God is, it is time to tie down a few concepts about His character.

Concept 1: God is Trustworthy

God is honest about himself and anything He does. He does not deceive, cheat or steal and so He is very reliable. He is reliable because He is a God of His word. He does what He says He will do. He stands by His word and insists that we remind Him of his own words.

Concept 2: God is Caring

God is compassionate and we see how He showed His compassion through the death of His only Son. In fact the Bible tells us that God's hand is not short to save us. He showed that He cared for mankind and when Jesus was on the earth He demonstrated this same compassion. He is kind and caring. He shows understanding by treating us with kindness, compassion, generosity and forgiveness.

Concept 3: God is Fair

God plays by His rules. These rules are the same rules we have to play by. He is fair with his to blessings and curses. He set before man life and death from which to choose. Each of these have rules that govern them. Yet He allows us to choose what we want and be responsible for our actions. A big demonstration of His fairness! He forgave us of our sins to be shabbily treated and manhandled before being crucified. He never blamed us. He cooperates with us as long as we are in his will. He recognizes the uniqueness of each of us.

Concept 4: God is Respectful

God has always treated man with respect. We can see it in the respect he gave to Adam from naming the created animals to the good and bad choices Adam made. In fact, this is what Jesus demonstrated when he walked with mankind on earth. He gave respect to those who were even disrespectful to him. He established the golden rule: do unto others…!

Concept 5: God is Responsible

God takes responsibility for everything he does. He does what he is supposed to do. He keeps his side of the bargain (even though we fail to keep ours). He is accountable in his word and deed and has a sense of duty to fulfill his promises reliability, dependability, and commitment.

Concept 6: God Perseveres

God has and is always pursuing worthy objectives with determination and patience even in the face of our resistance to him.

Concept 7: God Reflects Integrity

God adheres firmly to his codes (moral, etc). He is trustworthy, honest and incorruptible.

The combination of these seven qualities is what makes God stand out. In fact as Jesus put it you give to people who cannot repay you. This means that it is easy to judge God's character by the way he treats us even though we can do nothing for him.

Chapter 4

God's Nature is His Principle

In chapter 3 I dealt with the nature and character and concluded it by tying down some concepts about God's character which forms the basis of character traits one might expect from God. From the human point of view as well as the spiritual point of view, character does not come cheap. At least you see that from the concepts in chapter 3.

But before you get confused let me quickly say here that this chapter is not about God's nature or character. It is about principles. To be precise it is about God's principles, principles in which we expressly find God's nature. Let us begin by defining what a principle is.

What is a principle?

A principle is a set of concepts based on one's belief and forms the basis of a particular cause of action. Thus the concepts become fundamental laws that one obeys and follows through towards the achievement of an end result. These concepts become values based on which one can build true character.

A principled person will therefore stick to his/her principles (values) through thick and thin and will go as far as sacrifice himself/herself rather than break the principles. Do you see God sacrificing Himself for mankind in order to keep His principle? Truly God is a God of principle. A principled person is always motivated by his/her strong personal convictions that are demonstrated through his/her actions. Do you see God here?

Living by principles has an advantage. It is the advantage of concepts. Principle unites concepts in one single unit. Therefore a principle is a single unit that covers a multitude of actions. For example, the principle of truthfulness applies to every type of situation. In all situations one must speak the truth. Do you see Jesus here? People wanted Him to stop saying that He was the Son of God to prevent Himself from being stoned but he would not do that. The bottom line is that one has to pay a price for the advantage of principles.

Several principles can be seen in the Bible. In this book I will pin down a few of them. Remember that each principle is made of concepts.

Principle 1: Abundance

Abundance means numerous, plentiful, ample or beautiful. It also means a fullness of spirit that overflows. This is one of the attributes of God. This principle can be seen in the fact that it is more blessed to give than to receive. You may wonder how you give rather than to receive. Jesus illustrates this very well when he used the sower who went out to sow seed.

In the book of Mark, Jesus gives us an account of God's abundant principle in action. He tells of a parable about a farmer who goes and sows seeds in a field. During the farming season in that part of the world, farmers plowed their land during the early rains in September and October, and continued at times up until the month of March. The farmer plows the farm using a wooden harrow (having a heavy frame with iron teeth) to go over and over the soil thereby breaking the ground. The farmer would then walk over the plowed area and scatter seeds from a bag. He may sometimes retrace the land with the harrow, or use flocks such as sheep or goats to tread the seed into the soil in order to give it depth in the soil. This was done so that the seed could grow and produce a proper harvest.

> **The sower sows the word. "And these are they by the way side, where the word is sown, but when they have heard, Satan cometh immediately, and take away the word that was sown in their hearts." "And these are they likewise which are sown on stony ground who, when they have heard the word, immediately receives it with gladness." "And have no root in themselves, and so endure but for a time afterward, when affliction or persecution arise for the words sake, immediately they are offended." "And these are they which are**

sown among thorns such as hear the word, and the cares of this world, and the deceitfulness of riches, and the lusts of other things entering in choke the word, and it becomes unfruitful." "And these are they which are sown on good ground such as hear the word, and receive it, and bring forth fruit, some thirty fold, some sixty, and some an hundred.

Mark 4:14 -20

What we notice in this passage is that giving produces abundance. If you give little, you get little. A farmer who also plants just a few seeds will reap only a small crop, but if he sows much, he will reap much. The second thing you notice here is that you can never out-give God. Once you give, God will multiply and bless you back so you will have enough for your own needs; but plenty left over to give joyfully to others. The third thing you notice here is that your giving begins an endless cycle of joy God gives to you. You receive and you give to others. He multiplies it as an additional supply and gives back to you. As long as you continue giving the cycle will not be broken.

In effect, it is the law of sowing and reaping. What you sow, you will reap. First you must prepare a good soil. Second you must sow the best seed. Third, you plant as much as you expect in the harvest. Realize that no smart farmer will plant the poorest seed in a poorly prepared soil. This is disaster. He will rather buy or select the choicest (best) seed, prepare the soil with the best equipment and fertilizers and then plant as much best seeds as he wants in the harvest. In other words he seeks the greatest possible return on what he put in.

In the abundance principle you don't fear so you begin to focus on only what you lack but rather be open to unlimited abundance and experience greater security and joy.

Principle #2: God Does Not Redo What He Has Already Done

All through the Bible a familiar principle used by God we clearly see is that whenever He speaks it becomes a law. You will never find God redoing what He has already done. There are two reasons for that, which we will closely look at in this chapter. Reason one: in the mind of God "*everything God say's is finished before it is spoken*!" God speaks of the end before the beginning and what He says not only comes out exactly the way He said it, but it comes out completely finished, *"I make known the end from the beginning,* (Isaiah 46:10 *NIV*). Many years ago I was asked "that if God knew that Adam was going to sin," "why didn't God just start all over again"? I thought to myself, that this is an interesting question, one that I had no answer to at that time. "Why didn't God just start all over"? Interesting as the question may seem, I had no answer to it. We all know that broken things are usually fixed or replaced. The purpose of fixing or replacing broken things is to make sure that it is as good as new or completely new. With the help of the Holy Spirit I later discovered that if God were to redo what He has already finished, than He would have to change His laws, which leads me to my second reason why God does not redo what He has finished.

The second reason is that when God speaks it becomes law to both His creation and to Himself. What makes God God is His ability to uphold and abide by His own laws. *When God made His promise to Abraham, since there was no one greater for Him to swear by, He swore by Himself* (Heb.6:13 NIV). *"So is my word that goes out from my mouth. It will not return to me empty, but will accomplish what I desire and achieve the purpose for which I sent it"* (Isaiah 55:11 NIV).

I've heard it once said that laws are made to be broken. Well, that may be for the rebellious minds, but not with God. God does not make laws to have them broken by Himself or His creation. God's laws are set in place as governing principles to *protect* and *bless* mans life. *"Whosoever shall obey My command shall be blessed,"* is a kingdom principle found in Deuteronomy chapter 8 and chapter 28. For God to change what He started and finished would require that he scrap or revise the laws He established already; *"For I Am the Lord and I change not"* (Malachi 3:6). God's plans may change, but His purposes will always remain the same, and thus we can be assured that His laws will never change once they are spoken or decreed.

Principle 3: Whatever you give God does not Return to You Again

Whatever you give God does not return to you again, is one of the most profound principles I have ever received from the Holy Spirit. Whatever God gives to you in return He does it using a method I call God's Method of Operation (GMO). This principle operates one way, and that's His way. Say, for example, you gave God $1.00, and you did it with the understanding of His abundant principle. According to His principle, He has to return it back to you at a minimum of *thirty fold*. Why? Well the minimum requirement of God's Method of Operation if understood, will not allow Him to start with anything less then thirty fold.

If we look again at the seeds sown in the parable of the sower in Mark 4:14 -20, we see that there was one seed that fell on good ground. That meant that it was properly prepared or we can say it was received with *understanding*. The scripture tells us that the people of God are destroyed for lack of knowledge (Hosea 4:6). Jesus said that *"It is God's good pleasure to give us the kingdom,"* that would include everything that comes with the kingdom, such as righteousness, peace, joy, wisdom and understanding, and how much we understand will determine how much we will receive.

> **And he said unto them, "unto you it is given to know the mystery of the kingdom of God, but unto them that are without, all these things are done in parables." That seeing they may see, and not perceive; and hearing they may hear, and not understand; lest at any time they should be converted, and their sins should be forgiven them.**
>
> **Mark 4:11-12**

Principle 4: God Can Only Operate By His Way

For anything to manifest it must be done God's way through God's Method of Operation. All things are best done when we adhere closely to God's Method of Operation. We can do things successfully when we adhere to God's methods. Our failures are due to our not complying with God's ways of operation. We learn this from studying farmers or the farming process. God's laws are strictly adhered to in crop growing. The seed is first placed in the soil. Life that was dormant in the seed is powered into action and the seed is caused to germinate; the blade, the stalk and the mature fruit. No human wisdom or power can change this law of germination and growth. There is a grave danger in applying all sorts of human means in anyway whatever to obtain results. Remember that results are best achieved when God's laws and conditions are obeyed.

Principle 5: God Does Not Keep Secrets

God's desire has never been to kept secrets but rather to hide things for the diligent seekers. Those that would seek Him would come to know and understand Him better. *God looked down from heaven upon the children of men, to see if there were any that did understand, that did seek Him* (Psalms 52:3). *He is a rewarder of them that diligently seek him* (Heb.11:6). Seeking entails getting a better understanding of what it is you are seeking. The more we seek God, the more we come to know His ways. The more we come to know His ways, the more we stand to benefit from His principles. We should expect increase, and multiplication, when we seek to know more about Him, because it is in His nature to give to those that ask. When we apply God's method of operation to our devotional life, and the amount of time we spend in His Word, and the amount of time we spend praying, and seeking His will for our lives. All of these things can result in an increase in both our personal and corporate necessities.

Principle 6: Understanding Brings Increase and Increase Gives Access to More

The need to understand God's nature and principle is critical to our purpose and destiny. The scripture says "*Give a portion to seven, and also to eight; for you know not what evil shall be upon the earth* (Ecclesiastes11:2). The kingdom principle of sowing and reaping is not only for our financial gain, but it can easily be applied to our talents, gifts and abilities. Take for example the parable of the talents. There was one that was given five talents, and another two talents, and another one talent. All said and done, the lord came for them to give an account of their stewardship. The one that received one talent did not understand his lord (*perceived wrongly*), and offered to give back the same talent he had received. The lord then took from him that one talent and gave it to the one who had doubled his talent to ten (Matthew 25: 14-30). The lesson to be learned here is that God takes offense when we don't invest what we have been given. Not only is it God's desire for us to have more, but He expects us to use what we have been given sovereignly by Him.

Those that received the talents did not earn them through work but was given to them as gifts. How a person chooses to use his/her talents and gifts, will determine the type of response they will get from God. There are many people that are talented and gifted in the world but are reluctant to sow their abilities into the kingdom. To them giving of their talents and gifts to the kingdom is a hindrance to their success. Christ said (to paraphrase) "*make friends with the world and not run from them*" (Luke 16:9), that you may learn to become more skillful in your gifts, talents and abilities. We should encourage the perfecting of the gifts and talents within others by learning as much as there is to know from the world, so that the kingdom of God may come into its fullest glory. *"If the iron is blunt, and he does not whet the mouths, then he must put more strength to it. But wisdom is an advantage giving success* (Ecclesiastes 10:10).

Many of our talented and gifted youth have given their abilities over to things that reduce and lower their standards as decent human beings, thus limiting their potential in order to satisfy and please society. They are misinformed in believing that God will take away the things they enjoy the most if they surrender their will over to Him. God's plan is this; give your talents, gifts, and abilities over to Him and He will "multiply the seed sown, and increase the fruits of your righteousness in return" (2Cor. 9:10). In other words God is a giver and not a robber. The key words in 2 Corinthians 9:10 is that *"He will multiply"*. The reason why most of the potential in the church lie dormant is because there is a lack of understanding of God's Abundant Principle. Paul said we are *"Always learning, but never being able to come to a full knowledge of the truth* (2Timothy 3:7). As I stated previously, and I will restate again God's nature and principles must be understood first in order to receive all that He has for you.

Chapter 5

Understanding the Ways of God

The greatest revelation a person can receive, is to understand the ways of God

Wisdom is supreme, therefore get wisdom. Though it cost all you have, get *understanding* (Proverb 4:7 NIV). The most exciting part of my relationship with my children is the fact that they are learning to understand me better every day. They have come to learn what makes me comfortable and uncomfortable, what my likes and dislikes are, and to some degree how I think. Our relationship has developed into an understanding of how we all feel and behave in any given situation. When someone tells me about my child's performance or behavior when I'm not around, I could immediately tell by their description that it is my child he/she is talking about. Why? The answer lies in the fact that I have come to learn and understand my child's behavior (nature). It is not mere speculation or assumptions, but what I have come to learn and understand through our relationship.

God is not interested in our assumptions about Him, or what we may perceive to be His ways of thinking, but rather for us to learn how He thinks and does things. When the Prophet Isaiah was told by God that "*My ways are higher than yours and My thoughts than your thoughts*" (Isaiah 55:9), God was not directly stating to Isaiah, that He had a superior level of knowledge than the people, because God does not need to brag about His superiority. What God was alluding to was that He wished the people would come to know His thoughts or let's say seek to understand Him better. We have to understand, that the fall of man through sin, has robbed man of the knowledge of knowing far more about God than what he knows today. Even what we have now come to know about ourselves is minute compared to what we could have known. This of course has left a huge gap between man and his understanding of his Creator, which has resulted in mans destructiveness behavior.

Establishing truth is the best avenue to getting good understanding and access to God's wisdom and revelation. Jesus tells that "the Spirit of Truth shall *guide* us and *show* us things to come, and when He comes, He will not speak of Himself, but what He knows and understands about Me (Christ) *paraphrase* (John 16:13). Paul later writes in a letter to Corinth regarding the Spirit of God in that He (Holy Spirit) searches the deep things of God and reveals the truth about God to us, so that we may gain a deeper understanding.

But we speak the wisdom of God in a mystery, even the hidden wisdom, which God ordained before the world unto our glory. Which none of the princes of this world knew: for had they known it, they would not have crucified the Lord of glory. But as it is written, Eye hath not seen, nor ear heard, neither have entered into the heart of man, the things which God has prepared for them that love him. But God has revealed them unto us by his Spirit for the Spirit searches all things, yes the deep things of God. For what man knows the things of a man, save the spirit of man which is in him? Even so the things of God know no man, but the Spirit of God

1 Corinthians 2: 7-11

Our knowledge of God impacts our performance

Think of the kind of impact we could have if we were to know more about God each day. God gave man authority over the earth, and along with that authority He gave man three assignments, to *govern, manage* and *enforce* his God ordain authority. This meant that man possessed the power to have total dominion over everything on earth. Whenever someone in the Bible demonstrated a thirst for the knowledge of God, they were given unlimited access to God's full abundance. It was as though they were given the "keys" to unlock kingdom doors. Whatever their need was, they just asked, sought and knocked and the doors were open! Keys are meant to give access to something and to lock things out. When Christ said to Peter "I give you the keys *of* the kingdom," He did not say the keys *to* the kingdom, which meant to get *into* the kingdom, but rather, now that he was are a part of the kingdom, he had keys to the doors within the kingdom.

> **And I say also unto you, that thou art Peter, and upon this rock I will build my church and the gates of hell shall not prevail against it. And I will give unto you the keys of the kingdom of heaven, and whatsoever you shall bind on earth shall be bound in heaven and whatsoever you shall loose on earth shall be loosed in heaven.**
>
> **Matthew 16:18-19**

All of God's children have been given access to the kingdom, but not all possess keys "of" the kingdom. It is because not everyone has sought to acquire the knowledge of the keys, and without knowledge you cannot access the information you would need to bring about a true impact. Our knowledge of God impacts our performance and our performance is supposed to transforms our environment. That is why the more knowledge Adam would have received from God the greater his influence would have been on the earth. In the final chapter of this book we will look at some of those keys, and discover how to have full use of the keys by tapping into God's full abundance. God would love to give us access to more if we would only seek know to more. "*Blessed are they which do hunger and thirst after righteousness for they shall be filled*" (Matthew 5:6). He promises to provide us with everything we need if we would seek Him first "*But seek ye first the kingdom of God, and his righteousness and all these things shall be added unto you"* (Matthew 6:33). How much more would you like to receive from God? Are you satisfied with what you have come to know about God? Or would you love to know more? Let me encourage you; do not be content with just knowing His acts as did the children of Israel, but seek to understand His ways as did Moses, and then you will discover a unlimited access of His goodness.

Chapter 6

The Danger of Misunderstanding

What you don't know can kill you

It is inconceivable to think that anyone can live his/her life without some understanding of the basic principles of survival. If one is to survive he must know by natural instinct or create the kind of environment whereby he/she can discover the tools necessary to survive. Jesus came proclaiming the Good News of the kingdom. Whether he preached to the masses or taught His disciples, he clearly repeated and emphasized God's way of thinking. The key to this was to understand God as He would have us understand Him. It has to be on His terms, conditions and level of understanding.

What is critical to this is learning to appreciate His principles. This will make our walk with him effective. By doing this we come to understand God's nature in turn His principles can have a greater impact on our lives when we practice them. Without a clear knowledge and understanding of God, then our walk with God becomes more of a religion and less of a relationship. Every long lasting, successful and sustaining relationship comes by way of understanding. The more you know about an individual, the more comfortable, and confident and committed you become to that relationship. It has always been the will of God that we come to know Him better and that we learn more about Him through His principles.

God's principles are a product of His nature.

"*For I am the Lord, I change not*" says God in (Malachi 3:6).

This scripture teaches us that God has an unchanging nature, which in essence means His principles never change. We can expect that His nature is unchangeable. This simply means that God's principles are constant in consonance with His nature. It is therefore important that we not misunderstand His nature.

Why is this critical? The answer is because man can think one way about God, and later come to realize that he has lived his entire life out of touch with God's true purpose for his life. How many times have we done something that we regretted, because we later realized it was totally opposite of what God intended for us, all because "we" had the wrong perception? What is even worse is when we live most of our life off of a misunderstanding that we thought was true. Only to find out years later that was never

God's intent. It would be wise then for us to keep in mind that God's nature will always remain, "the same today, yesterday and forevermore".

Individual understanding is important to God!

I am fascinated by the relationship that existed between Abraham and God and Moses and God. They were called friends of God because of their relationship. The relationship was very personal because they understood God very well. God admired Moses to the extent that He jumped to Moses' defense when Moses came under attack from his brother Aaron and Sister Miriam (Num. 12:1-9). God personally admired Moses' faithfulness towards Him. I believe this was because Moses *understood* God better than anyone else. God spoke of Moses as someone who knew and understood Him as He would have him to. This was accredited to Moses as knowing (*understanding*) the ways of God while the people only knew God's acts. *He made known his ways unto Moses, his acts unto the children of Israel* (Psalm.103:7). Having a clear knowledge and understanding of God, puts us in a better position to have unlimited access to His wisdom, revelation and full abundance.

No person can truly be faithful over something they do not have a clear understanding of. Understanding increases the value of a thing. This means that you cannot place value on what you do not know or understand. In essence, our inability to understand puts us in a place of non-appreciation of the value of God's Word or understanding His nature. This can limit what we can receive through His Word. Every person committed to impacting the lives of others must consider that the impact they make depends on their level of understanding.

The impact of the wrong perception

One of the greatest dangers to anyone is ignorance perceived as knowledge. Many times Jesus' greatest opposition came from those within the church who truly felt that they had a greater understanding of God than Him. There were several occasions when Jesus was shocked to hear from those who had been taught the law with great strictness but lacked true understanding of the law. A case in point was Jesus' encounter with Nicodemus (John.3:1-10). Jesus answered and said unto him, *"Art thou a master of the Law of Israel, and ye know not these things"* after stating that *"Nicodemus must be born again"*. There are, of course, many Nicodemuses in Christendom today. They have perpetuated a sense of comfort in knowing just enough or knowing everything. That is why the book of Hosea says that God's people are destroyed because of a lack of knowledge and because they have rejected knowledge (Hosea 4:6).

Wrong perceptions cannot stand up against the challenge.

Christ many times was confronted by religious people because of their perception of what the Word of God is. They often tried to challenge or tempt Him into contradicting the scripture. Jesus sometimes spoke with a surprising attitude. His behavior shows that they were without excuses, especially when He said "*Being the masters of the law, why do you perceive the word of God incorrectly?*" The statement *"Why do you perceive the way you do?"* clearly indicates that they had a wrong perception. It was their thinking that became their philosophy, ideology and concept and this led to many confrontations between Christ and the religious leaders.

I've discovered that religious thinking people are dangerous when it comes to interpreting the Word, and are mostly to blame for verbal confrontation among people of faith. The mindset of religion has become one of the greatest dangers to the church and humanity today. Religion is the cause of the many of the world's conflicts we face today. Religion is basically mans way of trying to fit God into a finite space. It is the many perceptions and different interpretations of God's Word that leads to the kind of immature behavior we are witnessing today among religious sects. For example the constant attack on the way some view worship towards God, some would say that only their way of worship is the right way and how they conduct their services is right. The way they preach and teach the Word is right, and anything other than their way deserves criticism. Religious people are constantly challenging one another. Their whole agenda seems to be to get their religious views across and accepted as the right way. Instead of trying to get a better understanding of what God meant in His Word, they fight! If we are going to perceive correctly, we must perceive facts, evidence, and truth, and the best way to perceive right is to have received it straight from the right Source, which is exactly where Christ received it. Wrong perceptions cannot stand up against the challenge, so, let us perceive with caution, knowing that whatever judgment we make, we will also be judged by same. **How do you perceive?**

Chapter 7

Keys to Accessing His Abundant Nature

Key One: God is a God of Abundance

As mentioned before in chapter 4, the abundant principle was spoken into every living thing. Whatever God said came to exist through Him. *"Through Him all things were made, without Him nothing was made that has been made"* (John 1:3 NIV). This implies that the amount of potential that is in everything God created is immeasurable, and without limits. Many times our request to God seems as though we are uncertain whether or not He can meet our request, or supply our needs. Our hesitation to ask gives the impression that we feel guilty in asking God for too many things and so we say things like "if it be your will Lord," never really considering what that may sound like to God. For example, "Lord if you can do it for me" or "if, it's not asking too much," "I would like to know if you would do this or that". Assume that you are a parent that had it all. Your child knows that he/she had access to everything you have. Yet he/she comes to you with a beggar's mentality to ask for what he/she needed. You would probably be offended, and question what was wrong with your child, "Doesn't my child understand he/she can have whatever he/she wants?" "All he/she has to do is ask!" Unfortunately, this has been the approach of many of God's children – asking God for just enough. When His word tells us he owns everything.

The first key to reaping God's full abundance is coming into the realization and understanding that God's resources can never be depleted, drained or exhausted. God is full of things our eyes have never seen or can imagine. Paul encourages the saints at Ephesus by telling them that his God's supply is far beyond what they could imagine; that God maintains an abundance that exceeds their capacity to receive. (*Now unto him that is able to do exceeding abundantly above all that we ask or think, according to the power that worketh in us* (Eph. 3:20). The verse speaks to us of an endless and depthless supply of God's provision to His children. God will always exceed our finite expectation of what He is capable of, because God is a God of abundance. This means He does not just meet needs but will always supersede. He and He alone can suffice our needs without any help from us.

> **Your mercy, O Lord, is in the heavens; and thy faithfulness reaches unto the clouds. Your righteousness is like the great mountains, Your judgments are a great deep, O Lord, You preserve man and beast. How excellent is Your loving kindness, O God therefore the children of men put their trust under**

the shadow of Your wings. They shall be abundantly satisfied with the fatness of Your house, and You shall make them drink of the river of Your pleasures. For with You is the fountain of life in Your light shall we see light. O continues your loving kindness unto them that know you and your righteousness to the upright in heart

Psalm 36: 5-10 NIV

Jesus said *"With God all things are possible,"* (Matthew 19:26). In other words don't limit yourself to what you can do, but rather what God can do through you. God has in store some things for you, that you neither thought were possible or thought to ask, yet they exist, and are prepared for you, if you ask. God will never become satisfied with you living an average life, but that you may experience life and life more abundantly. This can only be done when you take the necessary steps that are required to getting everything out of the life that has been destined for your life. Things like peace, joy, and prosperity, just to name a few. God wants you to experience heaven on earth as He intended from the beginning. He wants you to have abundant living (John 10:10), but even more wonderful then that, He promises to supply you with everything that pertains to life.

God is so full of abundances of love. His abundance of love causes Him to commit to loving you. He has an abundance of mercy, grace and kindness. His wisdom and knowledge runs deep and cannot be numbered (Psalm 40:5, 92:5). Everything you and I will ever need is found in His abundance. When you make your request known unto God, go boldly before His throne and embrace His abundance for your life. Never settle for less than what He has already promised you, and don't think to ask whenever you are in need, because He is the God of abundance.

Key Two: God does not think in less than or equal to terms but greater than terms!

When God created the earth and everything in it, He expected every living thing not only to grow, but to continually produce more of its kind. When God created the seed in the tree, His concentration was not on the single seed, but on the tree lying dormant within the seed, with the potential to produce more of its kind. God's thinking process was to provide all of the necessary elements and ingredients in the seed so that the tree can grow out of the seed. That way there would be more seeds to produce more trees.

> **And God said, let the earth bring forth grass, the herb yielding seed, and the fruit tree yielding fruit after his kind, whose seed is in itself, upon the earth, and it was so. And the earth brought forth grass, and herb yielding seed after his kind, and the tree yielding fruit, whose seed was in itself, after his kind, and God saw that it was good**
>
> **Genesis 1:11-12**

How God thinks is essential to our understanding of Him. This is because God does not think in less than or equal to terms but greater than terms. God's thinking is more on what will be rather than what is happening now. His perspective, is that the end result, must be and should always be greater then the beginning *"Let the end of a thing be greater than the beginning* (Ecclesiastes 7:8). Jesus affirms God's way of thinking "that the Father desires that we bare *much* fruit", which is what He purposed and planned from the beginning (John 15:4, 5, 8, 15).

God is always looking to draw more out us

God is always looking to draw more out us. That is why He created everything He did. The purpose is to keep man's spirit aroused by the wonders of nature, creation and the universe. Man can then provoke his curiosity to challenge himself in order to explore and discover more, and to tap into the potential God placed within him. God looks beyond the single individual to a generation. When God created Adam, he was not just thinking of one Adam, but billions of Adams from Adam. At the time God spoke to Abraham who had no children. In fact he and his wife Sarah had given up hope, but God insisted that Abraham begin to see what He knew, and specifically told Abraham "*Look at the stars, for the stars will be the number of your seed,*" indicating that Isaac would be the seed to the beginning process of multiplication and abundance.

> **And I will make your seed to multiply as the stars of heaven, and will give unto your seed all these countries and in your seed shall all the nations of the earth be blessed**
>
> **Genesis 26:4**

What does it mean, "God does not think in less than or equal to terms but greater than terms? The evidence is clear when we look at creation. All living creatures have within them, the potential to reproduce themselves in order to secure the survival of their species. There are times when one off spring may appear in a litter, but even then, there are still more inside of that one, that has not been seen yet.

Thoughts are the beginning process but they should never be the end.

In the mind of God information is processed, completed, finalized and finished before it is manifested outside. God may start small, but He's always thinking bigger than where He started. He may begin with five loaves and two fish, but His thoughts are to end up with thousands of loaves and fish. He may begin with a ministry of twelve, but His thoughts are to end up with millions more. He never thinks in terms of less than or equal to, but greater than. There will always be times when we may need to experience small beginnings. We should not despise small beginnings. Genesis chapter one verse one says "In the beginning God created the heavens and the earth." The original text, reads "In beginning(s), God created the heavens and earth." It is as if to say "God had more then one beginning in mind". I believe it's because God never thinks in terms of less than or equal to, but greater than.

If there can be more than one beginning with God, then there can be more hope for a better ending. The beginning of your life may have started out hopeless, empty and confused, but if you can trust God, He can give you a better ending than your past. God can place people in your future that can help you in the end to fulfill your destiny. There is a process whereby we all must go through to get to where God wants us to get to. Sometimes we may fall short of where we are going, because of loss of focus, and too much attention given to the things we encounter from the beginning. For example, failures and mistakes we've made. If God has restarted your beginning, He will also complete it. *"Being confident of this very thing, that He which has begun a good work in you will perform it until the day of Jesus Christ"* (Philippians 1:6). In fact He has already mapped out your ending from the very beginning. You may have started out with a lot of bad times in your life, but I want you to understand that bad days don't last always. *"And we know that all things work together for good to them that love God, to them who are the called according to his purpose"* (Romans 8:28). His promise from the beginning was that you will have a greater ending *"That your latter days shall be greater than that of the former"* (Haggai 2:9). Christ came as a "New" beginning for man, giving man another opportunity to have a new beginning and a greater ending of eternal life. Your life is destined for change, if you allow God the opportunity to make the changes. If He can change the beginning, then He most certainly can change the end. How? He said *"I Am the Alpha and the Omega, the beginning and the end"* (Revelation 1:8).

We can now better appreciate the principle "whatever you give God you will never see again" taught in chapter four as we look back. If you give God $1.00, and He gives you back $0.50, than He would be giving you back *less* than what you gave Him. If you give God $1.00 and He gives you back $1.00, then He would be giving you back *equal* to the amount you gave Him (remember *God will never give you back what you gave Him*). If you give God $1.00 and He gives you back $3.00, then He has given you greater than what you gave Him.

Key Three: When God's law is not known fully abundance is unobtainable

It was his first trip on a cruise ship that he had planned all his life and the day had finally arrived. To him this was a dream come true. One he knew he would never forget. He packed his bags and went off. Arriving at the departing dock, he was greeted by the captain who handed him his ticket. "Is this your first trip" the captain asked. With a big smile on his face

He replied yes! “Well, enjoy your trip” the captain said, and off he went to look for his cabin. With excitement in his eyes, and his luggage in his arm, he couldn’t wait to settle in and to see the rest of the ship.

That first evening he walked to the top of the ship, as he watched the beautiful sunset, and felt the vibration of the waves crashing against the ship. Off to his right he noticed many of the passengers enjoying themselves "eating, drinking and enjoying the best the ship had to offer. While they laughed, sang songs and danced the night away. He stood there thinking to himself, “how nice it would be to enjoy the fun, food and entertainment,” but felt he was only privileged to take the cruise with the ticket he had purchased for the trip. He returned to his cabin to eat the box of crackers he had brought along on his trip. The next morning and days after, all he could do, was just imagine, how much fun it would be, to eat and play games with the rest of the ships crew. Being very disappointed and displeased with his trip, on what he thought would be the most exciting time of his life. He went back to his cabin to finish off what was left of the box of crackers he had brought on his trip. On the final day of his cruise while the ship was returning to the dock, he made his way to the ships exist and was greeted once again with a smile. “Did you enjoy your trip? Asked the captain” “Everything went well except for the fact,” “I had only a box of crackers I brought with me on the ship to eat." Surprised by his response the captain of the ship said "Didn't you know that everything else was included with the trip when you purchased your ticket?"

This story has been the case for many of God's people. We walk around ignorant of our legal rights to getting any and everything we need from God. Though God has all that we need, He is not obligated to give His *full* blessing, if we don't do exactly as His Word says. Until we come to understand and appreciate His laws, we will never fully benefit from them. Jesus tells us that God wants us to inherit His kingdom. Jesus did not mean certain things only, but all that pertains to the King and His Kingdom. *"Fear not, little flock; for it is your Father's good pleasure to give you the kingdom"* (Luke 12:32). The catch is this - God fully blesses, on the premise of what we know, and *"when God's law is not known fully abundance is unobtainable."* To obtain all that He has for us we must again do exactly what He says, but also know what it is, He has said to do.

All of God's blessings are conditional

All of God's blessings are conditional, conditional in the sense that if we obey Him *fully* we shall reap His full abundance. Every command, every promise and blessing God has ever spoken, holds a condition. That if we obey He will without any uncertainty, bring us into His full blessing and promise. Has it ever occurred to you how two Christians can hear the same word from God, and only one will work with it to produce maximum results? I believe faith is a factor, but faith without some understanding can cause a miscarriage of blessings. Blessings come by grace, while favor comes because of understanding and grace. In the parable of the talents, two of the three receivers - the one who had received five talents and the one that had receive two talents - understood what they had and what they needed to do with what they had, and so they reaped the maximum results. The person that was left with one talent, knew what he had, but wasn't sure what to do with it. The substance was there, but how to maximize it, was not clear. Even though the scripture does not say in details whether or not they all were instructed or previously informed, on what to do with the talents. I believe the lord at least expected them to know what to do with their talents. Listen to what this lord had to say *"You should therefore have put my money to the exchangers, and then at my coming I should have received mine own with usury* (Matthew 25:27). It sounds as if he was indicating that they should have known the conditions to receiving talents, and what was required of them. When the lord took his talent from the one, he did not give it to the one that had four, but rather to the one that had ten. That's favor! The greater our knowledge and understanding, the greater the favor we receive.

He that cometh to God must believe that He is, and that He is a rewarder of them that diligently seek Him. (Hebrews 11:6). The condition to receiving a reward from God is that you believe in God and His Word. Many of God's people will never enjoy the royal feast that the King has to offer. They will never reap His full abundance of good health, joy, peace, prosperity and all the wonderful benefits that come with Him serving Him, because they have never truly taken the time to understand His laws and His nature.

God has no interest in keeping things from us. He first wants us to have knowledge before obtaining what we seek. Solomon admonishes us in Proverbs *"How much better is it to get wisdom than gold and to get understanding rather to be chosen than silver* (Proverbs 16:16). It is better to pursue wisdom and understanding, because wisdom teaches you how to preserve and maintain what you have. Many people have gained success without fully realizing (understanding) its purpose. As a result, they lack compassion for others. It has always disturbed me to watch people go after everything but the things of God. Many today are in pursuit of companionship without the knowledge of its purpose, and so they never reap the full benefits that come with the blessing of marriage. Many today pursue the pleasures of wealth without the knowledge of its purpose, which is to establish His covenant. They abuse, misuse, mismanage and misappropriate the blessings of wealth, and never get to enjoy what they have been blessed with. The pursuit of happiness is to know what you have, and why you have it. That is why knowing is never enough to God, you must always pursue to know more from God.

Key Four: When God's law is known and understood, full abundance can be reaped

Many people know and believe there is a God, but lack understanding of what His Word say's about Him. In chapter five, I mentioned the importance of understanding the ways of God. Though we are superiorly created above all species and life form, I sometimes wonder how much animals know and understand about their creator than man. When the Tsunami earthquake in 2005 hit Indonesia, killing over 200,000 people, it was reported that there were hardly any traces of dead animals found on shore. As if, all of the animals knew immediately where to go for safety. Some would call it animal instinct, because they have an intuition about danger and instinctively know what to do when they feel something wrong is about to happen. Or could it be, they posses some level of intelligence and understanding about certain things, which man lost during the time of his fall from grace? One thing is for certain, the animals knew enough to save their lives.

I believe man has fallen so far from his true nature that he must begin the process of rediscovering and understanding himself, and his Creator all over again.

It's called "renewing the mind!" In the book of Romans Paul makes a profound statement about the fallen state of man, and its effect on creation *"For the creature was made subject to vanity, not willingly, but by reason of him who has subjected the same in hope* (Romans 8:20). Creation was made subject to sin because of mans sin, but not willingly. Verse 8 of the same chapter says, *"For the earnest expectation of the creature waits for the manifestation of the sons of God"*. Thus implying, that there may have been something known and understood by creation, that man does not know now, because it was lost when he fell from grace. I believe in part, that it was mans understanding about himself, creation and his Creator. It is almost as if the verse is saying creation itself is waiting to see again what it has known and understood from the beginning. What does creation know and understand? I believe creation knows and has a better appreciation and awareness of God, but not in a sense of understanding how God thinks. Only humans are capable of communicating how God thinks, and it is humans that God intended to understand Him. The fact that people say animals can predict future events, tell us the future, speak on behalf of the deceased and be reincarnated as peoples ancestors show how far man has fallen because of sin.

It is true that the gospel is simple. Its simplicity has become a stumbling block to many and so it is difficult for them to receive it. It's mainly because of our failure to know and understand the real truth about the gospel. Take for example, something as simple as the wise men that came to Jesus when He was a child in the manger. Many of us have been taught or heard that there were three wise men that came to Christ and brought Him gifts. We have been told that the gifts brought to Christ as a little baby were before he was born. The truth about the story is that Christ was probably a young child around two years of age, and there may have been as many as fives kings or even ten, because the scripture does not give an account of how many. Our failure in seeking to know the full truth can result in missed opportunities to receive God's full abundant blessing.

Some find it easier to struggle with their salvation rather than living it out as a child of the Most High God. A relationship with God is a way of living, a life style, what we were created to do, which is to present our bodies unto Him as a living sacrifice, holy and acceptable unto Him as our spiritual act of worship. I have discovered that the source of most people's frustration stems from just knowing enough and not willing to understanding more. "When God's law is known and understood then full abundance is reaped!" To live and not know why (purpose) can be worse than death, because purpose is only fulfilled through living things, and if you are living without the knowledge of your purpose, then you become unfulfilled. Here's what Solomon had to say about the purpose for your life.

> **Live joyfully with the wife whom you love all the days of the life of your vanity, which He has given you under the sun, all the days of your vanity for that is your portion in this life, and in your labor which you take under the sun. Whatsoever your hand finds to do, do it with your might for there is no work, nor device, nor knowledge, nor wisdom, in the grave, where you go.**
>
> **Ecclesiastes 9:9-10**

Knowing is never enough. Knowing that there is a God or that God exists will never bring complete fulfillment. It took King David many misfortunes and mistakes before he finally realized he did not understand God the way he should. In his final days as king, while on his death bed, King David not only gave instructions to Solomon regarding the building of God's temple, but admonished Solomon to get a better understanding of God. All of David's life as a little lad - a sheep boy - he knew who God was. He had first hand encounter with the power of God when He defeated the bear, lion and Goliath. This is what King David said to Solomon.

> **And you, Solomon my son, know you the God of your father and serve Him with a perfect heart and with a willing mind. For the LORD searcheth all hearts, and understandeth all the imaginations of the thoughts. If you seek Him, He will be found of you, but if you forsake Him, He will cast you off for ever**
>
> **1Chronicle 28:9**

David emphasized that Solomon was to know and understand God and to serve him whole heartedly. It is to be done with a pure heart. Later in verse 19, David closes by saying to Solomon *"That the Lord made me to understand"*. Solomon's first request from God was, *"Give me understanding!"* (emphasis mine). Because of that request, Solomon became the richest and wisest man to ever walk the earth, and he achieved far more than his father David had ever achieved while ruler of Israel. It was his desire to know and understand more, that attracted God's attention. That God went on to provide him with abundance in everything he did not ask for. The Lord said *"You shall reap the full abundance I shall give you"* (emphasis mine).

> **Give me now wisdom and knowledge that I may go out and come in before this people, for who can judge this Your people that is so great? And God said to Solomon, because this was in thine heart, and you have not asked riches, wealth, or honour, nor the life of thine enemies, neither yet have asked long life; but have asked wisdom and knowledge for yourself, that you may judge My people, over whom I have made you king. Wisdom and knowledge is granted unto you and I will give you riches and wealth and honour, such as none of the kings have had that have been before you, neither shall there any after you have the like**
>
> **2 Chronicles 1:10-12**

I'm convinced that once we move beyond just the knowledge of God, to having a better understanding of God, then there will be no limits to what God will do for us, and with us and through us. It wasn't until Esther knew and understood why God placed her in the palace so that the Jews would be spared extinction. It wasn't until Jonah knew and understood the mercy of God that the people of Nineveh were spared the wrath of God. The difference between two Christians that have a desire to prosper is not their knowledge of God, but how well each one understands God's law of increase. Could this be also why one church that is 15 years old can have an annual budget of 3 million, and another church that is 15 years old has an annual budget of $30,000 understand less about God? Or, the church that is 15 years old with an attendance of 3,000 while another church of the same age has an attendance of 50?

You may have ministry or church, and are experiencing the latter statement above. Your ministry may be struggling financially or with growth. It is of great importance that you stop everything you're doing and reevaluate what you are doing with the knowledge you have. Do you have knowledge without understanding? Have you put limits on your understanding by trying to sustain yourself with only what *you* know? In order to reap Gods full abundance, you must seek to understand as much as you can about God and His laws. Stop trying to make a living off of what you know, but rather seek to understand how to live for God. Seek to know and understand God as your source of life, as Paul writes in (Philippians 3:10) and as John states in (1

John 5:20).They both agree that it is Christ that we should seek to know and live for.

Key Five: Full abundance is only obtained through the laws of God

The rich young ruler had a question pertaining to life and wealth, on what more was needed to get heaven's full blessing. Jesus simply said, "*Sell all that you have and follow me.*" This was a difficult thing for him, and so he went away unfulfilled. He was looking for full abundance outside God's law. God's law is that no man should have any other god before Him. That includes money, wealth, fame, a career, people and things. Things should never become the object of our souls, whereby we need these things more than God. As I stated before, God is not obligated to fully bless us if we don't do exactly as He says. The will of God is that He should satisfy our needs if we would seek to please Him. No man or woman can ever achieve ultimate satisfaction or success without a relationship with God. It is almost insane to believe that one can fulfill themselves or their destiny outside of a relationship with their Creator. Just look around you and see the number of people that have tried, who thought they had it all, when in fact they were only trying to replace emptiness and a void with things.

God never intended that man's ultimate pursuit be riches, but rather for man to seek Him first, and then

He would address mans needs and desires. "*But seek ye first the kingdom of God, and his righteousness, and all these things shall be added unto you* (Matthew 6:33). It is one thing to have outward success and not have inward victory. If we are to have much peaceful, happier and fulfilled life, we must consider the following questions.

1. *Why do I seek the things I seek*?

There is in every human being a driving passion and desire to pursue happiness, peace, dreams, ambitions, answers and an overall sense of purpose and belonging. It is a gift endowed upon us by God to pursue greater and better things in life. The average person today comes into a world struggling with two or more identities – In who they are, and who they want to be. Our lives have become one big merry-go-round, pursuing and discovering things that will answer the question *why*? One of the greatest tragedies in life is pursuing things without a cause because that sets up a pursuit of vanity. There are many people who enter into college in their first year not knowing what to do and so pursue any major that appeals to them. As a result they waste three to four good years pursuing a major they are only trying out. Maybe they were told or advised by someone that they could earn lots of money in that field. Perhaps they were influenced by their peers or parents to pursue that study. Or, maybe they never took the time to ask the simple question "why am I pursuing this?"

I recall someone once said to me "it is better to choose a carrier that will most likely be available when you finish college" "since that would secure you a job". How many times do we go before God to see what career He wants us to pursue? What if God's choice is not the career choice we made? A word of wisdom, "never read a book that doesn't stimulate the mind"; "never use a tool that doesn't work", and "never pursue a dream you don't believe in". It is better to understand what you seek and know why you're seeking it, than to seek something and not know why.

2. *Where do I begin?*

Patients who are in need of a physician when they are sick, in pain or injured discover that their physician's primary concern is not the pain, but the cause of the pain. Discovering the cause of the pain (source) increases the physician chance of better treating the patient, by accurately prescribing a solution to the problem. Life's frustration can easily be treated, once a person discovers the source of that frustration. Many times, it is identified by asking the question where? Where do I begin?" Genesis 1:1 shows us how God got started which is a suggestion to where we can begin. If you ever want to know where to begin; you must always go back to the beginning, or where it all started.

Many times we begin our day without first communicating with our Source. We make decisions on things such as jobs, careers a business without involving the career planner. Our plans are made and finalized without acknowledgment and participation of the One who holds the purpose and plans of our destiny. The first recommendation on where to begin would be with God. His plans must be fulfilled exactly, if we are to reap His full abundance *"Many are the plans of a man's heart, but it is the Lords' purposes that prevail* (Proverbs 19:21). *We humans keep brainstorming options and plans, but God's purpose prevails* (Proverbs 19:21 MSG). The key would be to acknowledge Him in all our ways, so that He can direct our paths. In Psalm 139 David writes that God has a book written on the life of every person. This would explain why He knows the number of every string of hair on a person's head (Luke 12:70). If this is true, then God has already mapped out a plan for our lives. With His plans come laws that we must abide by in order for the plans to be realized.

Almost every piece of equipment today comes with some kind manual or instruction guide which tells you how to assemble a product or piece of the equipment. It is only when all of the steps on each of the pages are done exactly that that piece of equipment is completed and ready to function. Each instruction page gives you a diagram of a sort which shows you how the finish product would be. Once you begin the process and continue with the instructions without deviating from the directions, you will eventually see the finished product. So it is with God, if we are confused on where to begin, then why not start from the beginning and follow His plans for your life?

Just allow the process to take place while you follow His instructions for your life. Keep to His plans for your life, and don't become impatient while waiting to come into your destiny. Just know that every page in life is supposed to bring you closer to His full abundance. It is only when we follow Gods law exactly that we can reap His full abundance. I pray that you embrace these keys, while you commit your life to a life of obedience, His laws and principles. Decide today that you will receive all that God has for you in this generation and become a testimony to generations to come. Live your life in abundance by tapping into all that God has for you. Be willing to commit yourself to gaining more knowledge and insight about God and His nature and how he thinks concerning His Kingdom operation. Discover how to better respond more accurately to His Word, and let your spirit strive for perfection as your Father is in heaven. Fulfill your purpose, potential and assignment, as you embrace the knowledge of His Kingdom, because the more you learn about God, the more you come to learn about yourself. Finally, be defiant in your pursuit to know more, by not ever settling with what you already know!

To request a complete catalog featuring books, video or audio tapes by Frankie Jackson, or to contact him for speaking engagements, please write or call:

Syracuse Salt of the Earth Ministries, Inc.
P.O. Box 292
Syracuse, NY 13207
315-423-3829

email: syracusesaltministries@yahoo.com